FANTASY
BEN FAMA

UGLY DUCKLING PRESSE

BROOKLYN, NY

2015

Fantasy

Copyright © Ben Fama, 2015

First Edition, First Printing, 2015
ISBN 978-1-937027-47-6

Distributed in the USA by SPD/Small Press Distribution
Distributed in Canada via Couch House Books by Raincoast Books
Distributed in the UK by Inpress Books

Ugly Duckling Presse
The Old American Can Factory
232 Third Street, #E-303
Brooklyn, NY 11215

Cover design: John Lisle
Typesetting: Don't Look Now!
Type: Scala Sans and Advent Oblique
Text offset and binding: McNaughton & Gunn
Cover offset and foil-stamping: Hodgins Engraving

Funding for this book was provided by generous grants from the Jerome
Foundation's FACE OUT program, the National Endowment for the Arts,
the Department of Cultural Affairs for New York City, and the New York State
Council on the Arts with the support of Governor Andrew Cuomo and the New
York Legislature. UDP is a registered 501(c)(3) tax-exempt nonprofit and
a member of the Council of Literary Magazines and Presses.

NYSCA
New York State Council on the Arts

jerome
foundation

NYCULTURE
CITY OF NEW YORK

ART WORKS.

CONTENTS

FANTASY

Bruce rarely buys anything, fearing that one purchase will lead to the next and so on—like S/M where you must always raise the ante to achieve the same degree of pleasure until you become a different person and not necessarily the one you intended.

— Robert Glück

SUNSET

you need to plan what to do when you encounter an active shooter situation. in your workplace and commonly visited public area, it's advised to plan now to increase your chances of survival. visualize and plan escape pathways, hiding places and available objects you'll improvise as weapons. act with aggression. you should escape if you can, avoiding public lobbies if possible. otherwise, hide. don't leave a secure room. blockade the door with heavy furniture, cover all windows, turn off lights. silence any electronic devices, lie on the floor and remain silent. if neither evacuating the facility nor taking shelter is possible, chairs, fire extinguishers and belts may be used to disrupt or incapacitate the active shooter by attack using aggressive force paired with yelling. commit to taking the shooter down. 95% of shooters profile as white males between ages 18–44. they've been in psychiatry, therapy and are actively maintaining a diary and social media blog. sometimes life is more like a movie set than reality. unfortunately, you need to be prepared for the worst.

sometimes you just need to buy something. life is full of responsibilities. joyce carol oates at the beverly hills hotel. i take a selfie of myself crying. for life i cannot access. offered to you as emotional currency. the most beautiful thing i've seen today so far is an online collection of fan art—drawings mostly, pencil sketches on notebook paper. stars from twilight. britney. credited to anonymous sources. i was pulling up directions when my phone died.

i check my klout score. klout amalgamates influence across a range of media networks. my score is down 0.04. i attenuate this anxiety with a one hitter, the neon purple bat. i know i'm in a film because i'm sitting beside normsies at lunch. boring, ambitious and cruel—power normsies i guess, they smile sheepishly before going on camera. "they got married and ordered the ikea catalog pages 25–27."

provoking american gender anxieties. non-identifying and slant in the simulation. a new feminism sent from the future. the invention of the teenager in the early 20th century: new laws protect against child labor, parents no longer pair children off for marriage at age 16, an increased age through which children must remain in school. leisure time. access to transportation and their parents' income. a post-war economy. high speed and moonlight. freud's libido in the mainstream. dating. paraben-free barr-co oatmeal moisturizing cream. an off-the-shoulder sweatshirt in bleached turquoise. top of the bra showing. u look good bb. u look great.

a story about the body: they left for beach week on friday morning and stayed almost a month; brad paid for them with his dad's credit card. the game on the drive out is finishing a thirty-case of miller cans before they get to the cottage. they'll be drunk many afternoons living quite carefree in a crude paradise. summer passes this way. one day brad announces he's determined an unconscious festishization of kelly's body parts based specifically on where he finishes. dawn denounces this as the normalization of misogyny and degrading porn culture. brad says kelly's willingness to accept a facial is an intensely powerful source of affirmation. dawn says it is simply not true and greg adds that nothing is more politicized in sex than where the ejaculate lands. kelly flippantly says she actually likes it, which dawn takes as tantamount to violence against women.

it's a very sad thing to only look like a celebrity. sometimes, commuting from monica's apartment in crown heights back to mine closer to downtown, its easiest to get off at atlantic terminal. walking from the 2 line to the open air, passing the long island rail road tracks, and the schedule of times and the far away place-names of long island's east end: patchogue, bellport, southampton, bridgehampton, amagansett, montauk. it's an unexpected joy. marcel proust looking at a train station timetable and destination names says: *i had accumulated there a store of dreams, those names.*

he had the same feeling the first time seeing gilberte as a child, in front of a hedge of pink hawthorne, beside the steep little lane that led up to the méséglise way.

another violent news cycle this week. you'll wanna be high for this. a chevy blazer playing eminem passes the apple store on 14th st. did you see that email? people are writing *the worst* poetry. that apple store in chelsea services the hundreds of small galleries running mac minis looped into lcd screens. it's a clinton boom-era throwback economy. andrew tells me britney's breakdown in 2007 had a big emotional impact on him. old dreams waiting to be realized. pop culture displaces the threat of other discourses by not acknowledging them; a totalizing gesture. but just to be there.

someone was telling me about this bar called piranha. i've been meaning to check it out and go there alone. i've taken too much adderall and don't feel tired and need to engage with culture. i'm too late though I guess since it's half empty but i stay. stoli is on promo 1–4 am so i'm drinking. most people here are, like, networking. i read today there is a chance that our universe is a computer simulation. that theory is under investigation. understanding that if a culture could replicate a universal consciousness—our world—in simulation, it would. i drink and think about that. the dj is playing some really strange dance music. alien siren songs. as if brian eno's apollo soundtracks and atmospheres were re-written to reflect the darkness of our universe less understood after another quarter century of investigation. the 21st century and mtv's reification of despicable humanity and unending praise for the situation as it stands. the future inscribed in daily life.

at a video press conference broadcast from her floating home sanctuary off the coast of capetown in 2021, angelina jolie, alongside her family, announced that the majority of her body's cellular makeup had now been replaced by *accellate*, an artificially intelligent organic cell compound capable of regenerating major tissues, organs and bodily systems. from cellular respiration to major digestive functions, *accellate*'s "smart cells" decompose primary structural components of diseased and cancerous cells, removing them permanently, replacing them with new healthy "smart cells." "smart cells" also defeat typical organ decay in advance of aging and heal injuries at twice the human rate. the body will now continuously reconstitute itself. the eventual implications for endemic disease control are paramount. the public reaction was split. fundamentalists decried jolie for using her wealth to surmount death and god, liberals pleaded for *accellate* research to be released from the private market to the public good. not announced at the time of the conference were other leading *accellate* clients, including aids, animal and human rights activist ellen degeneres, and l'oréal fortune heiress françoise bettencourt meyers. also omitted was the fact that to date *accellate* treatment has shown no efficacy in male bodies.

you're at the grocery store when this next thing happens, that key foods on ave a that everyone wrote about in the '80s. you're already done shopping when this song comes on the speakers, "a trip to your heart." a track buried late in the 2011 album *femme fatale*, "a trip to your heart" is a luxury item servicing a mass audience, much the same as how fran lebowitz noted coca-cola is the summer house of the poor. the song starts out glitching as if to announce the execution of practical exigencies that make life so dreadful, displacing individual sadness and lack of validation. it's through cultural products like this that violence and self-harm announce themselves when youth culture tests its desires inside the *cultural poverty of a thoroughly franchised landscape*. britney inaugurates a temporary kingdom of pleasure, and her troubled history makes her a cipher you can't erase. britney. marcel. the weeknd. i'm going to miss you when you rebrand. palm trees pulled upward in a constant state of abduction. loft music. brian wilson. in the shadow of young girls in flower. john ashbery. i'm going to miss you when you rebrand. i'm going to miss you.

BOO

When a stereo goes by playing *Real Love*
that's when the revolution begins.
The whole boatload of sensitive bullshit.
When I lost my virginity I was thinking about
Wednesday Addams, from the Addams family.
No one probably ever called her boo. That's sad.
My boss keeps saying ICP to someone on the phone.
Indian summer sun falls inside this perfect soda.
Filmmaker Kenneth Anger...not in the one 1%?
Jeff Koons? My friends are in this band called Damien Hearst.
I love reality but there's no money in it—I wrote that because it's true.
Remember 2011?
The year Amy Winehouse died of a broken heart.
And Four Loko became illegal.
Somehow my childhood cat died.
One of the first images of utopia I saw was the MTV video for *Today*
by the Smashing Pumpkins. It's inconclusive whether the bread truck
they drive is running on vegetable oil, though the whole video
is basically a depiction of the art-as-play narrative
post-modernity rescues through Nietzsche,
or, as Adorno said, an impossible-but-necessary image of liberation.
If Snooki were my daughter, I would not be proud of her.
Let me give you a second to tweet that.
When I die I want my ashes scattered into the twin waterfalls
of a hotel named The Salish.
I've left the details with Jesse because I trust her to deal with this
in a way so as not to profane grace. That sounds like something
Larry Levis might have written. Larry Levis died in Virginia, at age 44,
where I was born. When I was 25 I was going to move to Portland
to join a bike gang I'd read about online. Also I thought my 'zine

could really thrive there. Jesse lives in Portland and has a more
sophisticated phone than even I do. All phones are basically smart
because they continue to function while I am ridiculous.
When I'm terrible, that's when Jesse's cool.
It's 85 degrees today in October
a Sunday, much hotter than Fall felt in the catalog.
A day after Christopher gave the eulogy at his mother's funeral,
which I have forgotten about. I only remember because I called him
for something too small or unimportant to write here.
He was about to get on a bus to go upstate.
Later I saw a picture he posted of this lake—it was seemingly endless.
The sky golden brown and pink,
a gradient of makeup like you could see at the ballet
I don't know what to say
of the works and women I loved
when I knew less.
Some I still do.
There's not much I believe in.
Things I can be present inside.
A sample sale.
What's new for Fall?
Maybe "sample sale" is the best phrase, not "cellar door,"
which is supposed to be phonoaesthetically perfect.
The sharp "a" in "sample sale" breaks the space
making capital's entrance
in this otherwise innocent moment.
I'm aware I am using the rhetoric of Christianity
to attack an economic philosophy.
Where is Feminism now?
Feminism is so fucked right now.
I want Rei Kawakubo to be my mother.
Her eternal black pitch.

As if the cedilla hanging down from Comme de Garçons
(it looks of course like an asterisk or the anus)
is the black hole, or degree zero I was born of
wherefrom passes the structure
of avant-garde capitalism along with its concomitant critique.
When people talk about Fashion it seems so gauche.

FUR

I see fur
when I cry

in the piss
of a queen

when I lie
and it's liked

in the sky
when you text

ANAIS NIN

My 1L is falling apart
is that a good wig
or an iPhone app?
the decade is pixels
endless scrolling
everything before
was glitter
the internet is one of my
major erogenous zones
false eyelashes, nail art
I just licensed
someone else's art
to Forever 21
in this virtual open world
I'll never work again

LOS ANGELES

Like any subscription member
of the Metropolitan Opera
fashion bloggers believe
they're at the center of perception.
I want to go where men go.
Is a high school crush
on an alien surf girl
the same as the need
to fatally possess
the other and the self?
My friends were in a band
called Second Life®.
Let's get high
talk about '90s nostalgia
Scientology
drink Diet Coke.
The Real is a teenager
drunk in a turn.
A blue dot pulsing down
Santa Monica Blvd.
Hackers are the
unacknowledged legislators of the world.
For something to be timeless
it must be outside mortality
and if humans exist outside of death
they're no longer subject to the violence
of sexual reproduction
or the fragility of life itself.
In these conditions music
will have no cultural efficacy.

Hope life now won't need.
A forever sadness, though possible, now obsolete.
What did I do this weekend?
Listened to this song "Tropical Winter" on repeat
while POV jogging through Runyon Canyon.
Totally desperate boys following cute boys
making out under Tumblr skies
reblogged as gossip
sent from my iPhone.
Kenneth Anger fatigued and
decadent in silk
post-fantasy.
Negation is part of the
positive identity of an object.
There is no snow in Hollywood.
Celebrities constitutive of a
scene that draw the populations
restaurant owners want as their clientele.
In a single day three stars photographed
in the same gray hoodie.
I want to create a product
too unstable to be marketed.
Not to say lacking
maybe messy
discursive and sort of pushing
oscillating among
the various dimensions of influence.
I could write here randy details
of my consumer choices
banal and otherwise
it would not amount to much.
Mallarmé on fashion.

Benjamin on fashion.
A monograph retrospective
of Guess's photo editorials
next to the bed.
So maybe alien visitations
directly influenced human history over the millennia.
What does it take to start a new life?
You take lonely trips to the city
you are interested in moving to.
Saturate the market with your resume.
During interviews order both coffee and juice.
Masterfully handle the acceptance of your ontological incompleteness
by affecting the persona of the applicant they want to hire
a winning assurance that you never intend to realize
obvious to all parties six months into the job
as if persona or voice was something laid stable
over the truth of a tectonic subjectivity
Jean Paul Gaultier staged his Chic Rabbi
collection at Paris Fashion Week FW '93
Very beautiful, very elegant, the orthodox religious
clothing and the gender bending
fits with his interest in tradition and iconic imagery
as well as the fact that he's treating somewhat impertinently
something that most people wouldn't dare play with
in couture design.
When Gaultier talks about himself though he sounds so dumb.

FANTASY

Forever is the saddest word
The poem's not worth it
I'd like to read to you
What Andy Warhol said
About the traps of the rich
But my tastes are changing
This is a love note
To a Fire Island lifeguard
Tuscano shearling
And mauve champagne
I should never talk
Even after two sips
Though that's when I can
I hate the George V hotel
But I would take you there
Then walk to the open market
Some thoughts are not that great
The Internet is my home
Where it's easy to be beautiful
And seen and new
In the glow
In the spell
I thought I was better
I guess I won't ever be
God wants us to make out
'Cause I'm in this airport
Where nobody's important
I just wrote a letter
Explaining all of this to you
In my head

The prism refracts
But the stone is cloudy
All that comes through
Are the deeper obsessions
Arvid Nordquist and dry shampoo
Cocaine and Pellegrino
This weather should have an entry
In *A Lover's Discourse*
A fully enclosed private garden
With direct access to the pool
Hardwood floors
Perfect light
I, like, crave you
Doesn't it ever just make you sad
Plans you had with different people
And how it all can't come true?
I want the extremes
Of pleasure
Boredom
Watching my lovers cry
I really want to show something
To the lifeguard from Fire Island
Thoughts like nectar
International cities
To stand here a young prince
Unique in spirit
Replete with hospitality
Aren't you even curious
To see my hotel room
After I swim?
Sitting on my bed
I typed

Principal Dancer
Into YouTube
And drank
To see the discourse
And the honor
Feels good
Standing at my window
What I think I will miss most
When I die
Is color
And the light
Sometimes it just comes to you
Amidst occasional instances
Of radiance or darkness
I mean
Everyone has their shit
Then enough time goes by
That's your life
Maybe I expect too much
I wouldn't know how not to
In my room
With these portraits
In gold frames
Feels like theater
MGM Pictures
The bronze light of Hollywood
1928
The future isn't real
I should walk in golden rays
Past rows of motorcycles
To Coney Island
Because I know grace

Is more real than love
It feels so real
In the morning
On Fifth Ave.
With the lifeguard
From Fire Island
Weightless in badinage
Whatever comes from
Art and life
Being can be too easy and common
Like soda
I let him come inside my world
Because they gave me a key
To Gramercy Park
Maybe tonight
I'll have a breakdown
Sometimes
I use this French product
To soften the water
When I soak in the bathtub
It is silent there
Like a tomb
Sometimes I wish
I was already in mine
Sometimes I wish
The world had a face
I could touch the cheek of
When I feel
I could be a part of it
When I cannot
And I lie in the hot water
Sometimes I wish

The pearlescent steam
Could sublimate the malaise
And the lassitude
That is there inside of me
Maybe it does
I believe it is that way
When the light touches down
Upon bunny lawns
Of Fifth Ave.
I don't care at all
About the lifeguard so much
Gravlax or Paris
I should call this friend
In Los Angeles
An aesthete who hosts parties by the pool

ELLE

i would
make out
with you
hold hands
smoke weed
etc

HUNNO

After Bunny Rogers

the world is yours
60# gloss pages
pop stems
Nicki
listen to my heartbeat
on Sunday
I cry for the beach
why do people say
I just hate celebrities
rather than
It's smart to recognize
exemplary moments?
a bad table at Spago
late nights at Katsuya
the cute couple from
that pay-as-you-go site
"Come over
at do bring coke now"
we'll complete this study
in hate, or self-hate
illusions of boyhood
LaTurbo Avedon
wrapped in code
sometimes tilted blinds
slot jade shadows
on my wall
the millennia turn
a shout from the woods

a frat house in full sun
fucked up my Warhol like
the world is yours
you can go to the Met
to hear music and drink
four Beefeater martinis on credit
with a Lillet rinse
and a pickled baby onion
kiss me a final sunset
April folds its snow
you are shitfaced
and find a place
to lay down in the park
you fall asleep
and someone steals your backpack
but only your work computer was in there
I'm just a California boy
having two or three people in love with me
like having money in the bank

SNO-CONE

pics or it didn't happen
sort of hot girls
wearing Toms
other normsies

I'm behind a curtain
in a car
spending money
on Amazon.com

I get into the culture
of attention
elegiac pixels
an exit strategy

I'm Abercrombie
at the bus stop
completely lost
pill regimens

young and hungry
for new presence
this great sports club
at the next turnoff

I am a perfect person
more lace than sole
Giuseppe Zanotti
pride of an empire

I'm smart
as smart as Siri
chatting teens on Grindr
drunk in the sand

this critic says the work
was "Ikea-friendly"
I laughed and I don't even think
that phrase means anything

on Hollywood I was trance
my iPhone autocorrected
soulmate to *simulate*
we split an Adderall

in the mood
aliens watch you fuck
large oval eyes
reality is a buzzkill

ODALISQUE

There's a picture of you on my phone
I look at when I'm bored
It's basically an American Apparel ad
In a world I have access to
I'm looking at it now
Or possibly through it
And listening to "Gymnopédie No. 3"
Sometimes I think it is a perfect song
I wonder what you are going to wear
To this cocktail event
At the Gershwin Hotel
We are going to
But when I left you were sleeping
And I don't think you are awake yet
It becomes obvious
When I am thinking of you
Lying on the bleached sand
In the soft powdery
Easthampton light
I will die
Under conditions
Premeditated by myself
I think in that eyeliner
Lancôme and Dior
You would give me
Something to live for
By doing something
Remarkable
Like throwing
A champagne flute

Off a yacht
Making me
Want to throw you down
Against the hard-packed sand
The Amagansett waveline
Until all that is left to feel
Are the elegiac melodies
Nocturnes rapt in the air
I should hire a painter
To capture this feeling
So that we may simulate it again
Before returning to quiescence
Today it will rain
I should take you into town
To the galleries
In a Japanese yellow raincoat
To have some champagne
At a group show of landscape paintings
I'm sorry they will probably be shitty
Driving back to New York City
Mendelssohn, Grieg, Liszt
It is Memorial Day
Drinking grappa on ice
From a plastic cup
In traffic
I think I left my magazine at the beach
If you were not here
I'd be incredibly bored

FLÂNEUR

Fashion makes me less crazy
It should be looked at
Never discussed
It's an honest joy
To be shocked by beauty
In the 21st century
I was shocked when my lover was caught stealing
From Dean and DeLuca
I was thinking of a line
By Robert Hass
The floor manager stopped us
We simply went to a different store
Poetry
A requiem for leisure, pleasure, thought
I cannot take your high school friend's
Hoop earrings seriously
And every picture on my phone is obscene
Look at it
All these effetes
Boring travel stories
Details of somebody's dreams
Champagne condensating
On leather seats
All summer long
I wish I could afford a room
At the Peninsula New York
Suites with TVs above soaking tubs
With city views
And all that sun on Fifth Ave.
I live inside it too

I am at Uniqlo
Buying underwear
And after I paid
I stayed and shopped again
A surprising second erection
After you've just finished
And you know it's time

MEXICALI TWINKS

trust me
celebridades
natsume nana
anorexic girls
trying for a baby
curvy mature
public no bra
real teens
under blanket
goth girl
ballet boots
coquin de france
amateur teen couple
amateur facebook teen
lana loves it
love on a plate
electrician
emo twinks
anime pregnant
chubby swinger
webcam gold show
tail plug
bikini squirt
my mom's friend
nick in the office
keeping job
kitchen counter
prolapse eating

PEARL LAKES

There are things
You can't get anywhere
But we dream
They can be found
In other people
No one can fuck
With my love
I'm on this boat right now
Kylie Minogue's *I Believe in You*
Is coming up from the cabin
Off an iPod dock
Bobby's talking about his next tattoo
I'm thinking I wish Claire
Had actually died
I'm in the sun
We're both smashed
All I did was to come to a funeral
And it's like I fell into a dream
To live among the orchids
My last gift to Laura
Who hasn't
On an awkward night alone
Laid back and pleased themselves
Thinking of the girls at Horne's perfume counter
Their slim fingers
The make up tones
And that one soft true thing
Or the disgusting and sweet leather
Of Bobby's jacket
Or James's

If you like guys like that
Did I read somewhere
That Special Agent Dale Cooper
Was basically a Boy Scout
From the dog star Sirius?
Or how David Foster Wallace said
If you're ever in a situation
That evokes the capacity for feeling
David Lynch creates
You should get out of that situation
As soon as you have the chance
I think
David Lynch
Creates worlds
That are not like our own
Which is not the way television is supposed to work
Usually you have a soft abstraction of everyday events
Detached enough from reality
Canned to be like the lives we live and breathe in
The deviations therein hold our interest
I believe
In dark magic
And the dark woods
And the times our real lives
Mimic the currents of Twin Peaks
Cause dread and uncanny temperament
In the self
Anyways
My mom use to watch this show
Unsolved Mysteries
And this one particular scene
From April 4, 1991

Showed 20-year-old
Bank clerk and college student
Angela Hammond
From Clinton, Missouri
Getting abducted while talking to her boyfriend
On a gas station payphone
There were long shots
Where the viewer saw her
Freaking out when she realizes
This guy in a truck was waiting for her
The boyfriend she was talking to on the phone got in his car
This station wagon—you can imagine—
And tried to find her, and he did find her
Cause in this small town there was no one on the streets
He heard her scream
When she passed him in the abductor's truck
So he chased them for a few blocks
They showed the girl struggling with this guy, the kidnapper
His truck had a decal across the small windows
Behind their heads
Of a fish jumping out of water
A detail that was backlit by headlights
And pressed upon my unconscious
During this dramatization
They even played this shrill, slowed down version
Of a woman screaming
Basically just like Maddie Ferguson dying
But anyways, the station wagon
Died out during a shift into reverse
And they never found the girl
When I was a young teenager
Buffalo Bill was the scariest villain

I'd seen in a film
I didn't know much
About drag culture then
To realize it was camp
The best part
About writing a poem
For Twin Peaks
Is that
There already is a poem
In Twin Peaks.
We hear it from Rita Hayward
Donna Hayward's little sister
Right after the youngest Hayward sister
A piano prodigy
The real baby of the family
Performs in a pink tulle leotard
And rhinestone tiara
She'd make the perfect internet girl

NORMSY

I didn't know you were such a normsy. You don't even know who Joy Division is. And you always like the boring parts of museums. I didn't know you were such a normsy.

FRANK O'HARA

The only time I wish
other people heard my thoughts
is when I put your name
into youtube.com
right now I'm thinking
I wish you were still alive
so I could be your partner
whether in art or life
I'm not really sure
mostly life I think
but they say
life imitates art
so who knows

GIRLWITHCAT2.JPG

I found you
on Gothtrash.com
and saved your picture
to my computer desktop
it gives me the feeling
of something terrible
and familiar
a space
between lives
like seeing Marcel
seeing Gilberte
for the first time
how the fact of life itself
becomes a thing
languished and melancholy
I think I would like to lie
among southern magnolias
in snowfall
dark skies above
into which
I will never enter
I'm watching Maya Deren
maybe I will smoke weed
I called out sick
it's the afternoon

MOËT

The Rodarte sample sale was shit
Now I'm just lying on my sofa
I hate this "in love" feeling
But I have it

#NOFILTER SKIES

sunset me
Pouilly-Fuissé
a postcard in the mail
from Burbank, California
even my own thoughts
I think only somewhat
Haribo gummies
girls in fall clothes
I'd like to perform something
not dominated by industry
each consumer decision
is a chance to end the world
an expense report
celebrities vacationing
in sunny Polynesia
teens smoke salvia
in the Ikea parking lot
call your girlfriend
it's time you had the talk
now is a good time to start reading
a book called *Dead Souls* by Nikolai Gogol
on our second date
we put up this Hemnes wardrobe
there are exotic myths
that have to do with size
anorexic pool boys
serving hot dogs
in the nude
I forgot the things he said to me
a Polish working class guy

who went to Fordham
looked into the dark waters
considered suicide fall semester
a creep in an idle Honda Zipcar
in the parking lot
just staring
W Magazine
I dream all night

R.I.P.

I don't want to
be on an island
without celebrity
or flirt
sea like a mirror
I don't know
if I'll make my link
it's basically Monday
I think on the island
yesterday a horse died
right there at the party
and the girl was so sad
with a braid in her hair
her birthday is Getty Images
I show her some
I don't know
how it is
beneath the sand
it's sad
to know so little
like this island
it's perfect
to wave your nudity
from the end
you find something
send it to print
it's totally fine
like the potion
if it's good
you breathe it in

I have
Sandy missed the link
I said it's ok
I mean whatever
I start feeling bad
and walk to a new location
and look through magazines
until I'm ready
to respond
I'm not too famous for it
it's just this reputation
around the island
I have nothing
you know that
I could kill
you told me
everyone agreed
at the party
I wasn't there
Sandy was
sort of waiting
alone in curls
there was a singer
slow and elegant
she texted me
I couldn't respond
I was in public
I had no thoughts
other than people
uglier than me
getting fucked
at that moment

I'm not afraid
of falling in love
some die
Claire did
I thought
I saw her today
in the metro
my heart went crazy

LIKE

There are some feelings I'd like to demonstrate
To a woman of my age
I know you about 3%
We've hung out
Then you moved to Los Angeles
Thank you for accepting my invitation to chat
I like your hair
I like your shirt
I like how you have a funny picture of Justin Bieber in your online photos
And some sexy ones of yourself too
Are they ironic?
They're good
Have you ever had sex outside?
Is there a relation between the internet and madness?
Perhaps this video chat application will provide a forum for us
To further explore this question
You will not be upstaged

I'm sad a lot

I'd like to get away from culture

Are you staying with anyone?

I have these records...

There are a few things I know by heart

Today I had to look up the definition of perfidy

And louche and remembered

Things said for Art always sound true and aren't forever

Dark all day

Glamour all night

Public makeouts

Unsolved celebrity murders

Tabbed browsing

Cubicles

Love me or not

You'll be sorry all fall

Have you met my housekeeper?
I was touching you and you said not too much, that was it
The balcony windows were open and we slept
Someone put peacock feathers under the door
But there are still things I want more of
So you live in California
We meet in a hotel room
VH1 plays in the background all night
No compromises are necessary
Just ride it out
Express wave
Basically I'm wearing shorts
And there's a lot of white girls

I want a blonde more than I want my next book to be pink
Loveless
Sometimes I feel that way
Did we have a good time
I'm here
You're just leaving Soho?
Wanna come to Chelsea?
I am
I'm going to Boston tomorrow morning...
Do you know anything about car insurance?
I may be driving a car?
My friend Lindsey says hi
I need a cocktail now

I think I'm in love with the world of billboards and magazines
It is so intrepidly based in fantasy
Like things online
And literature, all the immaterial world
I mean the actual world we live in all the time
Like mp3's and visual art
That replaced painting
I dunno
You're the best actress in the world
Right now you are acting retarded
Your agent comes in on roller blades, wet and horrible
I like it
I'm gonna go shopping all afternoon
Then I'm gonna need to have sex with someone
Let's talk about it in the car
This work will not last

I think the invention of the alcoholic energy drink *Sparks*

Was the event that launched the 21st century

Not 9/11

This is some really good music

If Frankenstein was in a really good band it would sound like this

I was alone on the beach thinking about you like really late last night

If the world ends tomorrow I don't want to still be mad at you

Once I was dumped via email while I had an auto-reply response up

It took two weeks

For me to learn my new status

It was so sunny that day, I remember

I was drinking on the balcony of some house in Miami

You know how wonderful the 21st century can be

The details do not improve what's at stake here

Maybe this new profile picture will open some doors

I've been dying my hair black for 15 years

What's it like to be you?

That post on Deleuze started a fucking orgy

I don't even talk like this

You make me

I'm so obsessive

My car is beautiful

Antonio Villaraigosa calls me for advice

So we meet for lunch

I say

I'm not a writer

I'm a stylist

A charlatan

With an unwholesome interest in all people

He wants details

I'm ready to fall

For the subtle grace which I am able to describe you with

Soak a sugar cube in bitters
And place it in a glass
Fill the glass with champagne
The decade happens
You're not the only one I'll love
Solar plexus
I am evil in it
My life
Walk to the water
What's been done here will
Be relevant
I'm writing this so the youth may learn
The power that kills that they may live
Fama   Witchcraft   Ouija   The Valley
Muscular and romantic
I'm ready to fall in love
And envy the perfection of what I've done

Who will keep my secrets when I die?
I want to be shot with an arrow
Into a jacuzzi while the jets are firing
Boys
Girls
Pools
Human Sexualities
Suburban spells
I cannot numb these vulgar emotions
Maybe in a long email made of disabled things people say as "I"
Maybe you heard them
In the original French version?
As if falling in love were so uncool

I want a swan to spit an expensive Malbec
Straight into my wanton mouth
It's harder if it's true
I could make an enemy
I'd like to get involved
You can't die from loneliness
But can't I try?

Can your makeup remover do that?
Do you want to go to Dazzle Ships?
How are your Wednesdays?
Don't be such a guy
Aren't we all just looking for love?
Appearing in the element of pure presentation
I sleep beside this psychotic altar
My bedroom looks like a tomb
I want my headstone to say
stay cool
Or *have a nice summer*
Just being alive
Paying for things
Hanging around
Whatever
Contact information
White linen
Pre-cum
Prosecco
Kokomo

Whenever that song comes on, *Kokomo*

That's when the world begins

It's the kind of cultural production capable of dissolving

Any kind of human grief

Satanic physical allure

Tropical contact high

Diane Keaton young

Diane Keaton hot

Celebrity impersonators

Soba Noodles

Salmon Wraps

Sushi Rolls

I just had dreams so intense it's like a sea-wash over all reality

Like I actually had to remember the details of my life

As they came to me

Gossip is better than pornography

But they both make great screen grabs

It's not even 10am and you've already

Put Napolean Perdis foundation on top of

Dr. Macrene 37 Extreme Actives anti-aging cream

Doctor Dennis Gross Skincare Alpha Beta and

Dr. Brandt Time Arrest Creme, over a layer of

Neutrogena Ultimate Sport Sunblock Lotion SPF 70+

Bobbi Brown pink lipstick

MAC False Lashes mascara

Chanel eye shadow

Estée Lauder perfume

(a fragrance that cues remarks from friends and strangers alike)

Sonia Kashuk concealer

Bobbi Brown beach body lotion

And Bausch & Lomb contacts

Probably more coverage than you need for a plane ride though

I've gotten to read this poem in the garden

Of the Museum of Modern Art

At a remembrance for Frank O'Hara

In the summer of 2008

Even his sister was there, Maureen O'Hara?

Because I wanted a poem to fulfill all my needs

Death curious, a shy dirty mind

I've gotten my way for way too long

Though I would plié for a moment of your attention

Even if it's staged

Like performing sincerity

Which people have done

Since Revolution Summer in 1986

Do you have access to that?

Perfecting my tan in the backyard

Then writhing on a couch in front of daytime television

I just have a brain full of information

Your pictures haunt it

That makes them real

I wish I could stand behind them

But even that commitment could become

A limitation on the play I need

Basically I'm a 13 year old goth child

And when I picture the graveyards I imagine

Faces beyond the tallest spires and headstones

Nothing more remains except to know them and to love them

There are some feelings I would pay for

Because this tan can't last forever

Maxxis girls

New York Dolls girls

Yves girls

Art House Revival

Plastic looks

Long legs

Tomaž sends letters
Another day in this head
Over and over until you're dead
I got really fucked up at work

I've been working on this screenplay
And I'm impressed with myself—
A romantic comedy, for teens
Basically updating *Sleepless in Seattle*
And *You've Got Mail* for the social media generation
Where two people meet online, in the comments section
Of a pop culture website, and develop a relationship through
Online correspondence and text message
He's a writer living in Washington DC
Basically a hoodie heartthrob type
With a large friend group and some moderate successes
Who otherwise can't get his life together
She lives in Chicago and dreams of becoming a professional artist
Giving her life over to a day job
As the editorial assistant of a lifestyle magazine
Alluded to briefly throughout various points of the story
As *Teen Vogue*
Breaking into hotel pools with her girlfriends by night
She's a little wilder than he is
We hear her confide to her co-worker over the phone
That she is feeling lost in general
While his roommate in DC, the co-star of the film, is determined
To leak a sex tape of himself which will go viral
Launching his career as a web-age porn star
This virtual romance goes on predictably as life continues
Over short emails, texts, cute pictures
Basically just trying to share something with someone
Where is the strangest place you've ever masturbated, she'll ask
On the Ferris Wheel at Coney Island, he'll text back
She sends him a video of a student film she starred in during college
A remake of Francois Truffaut's *Les Mistons*, meaning *The Brats*
Where she rides around dirt country roads in a sundress on a bicycle

Eventually the protagonist's roommate uses our hero's cell phone
To send flagrant texts
Causing a meta-conversation, over a phone call
Which until now would have been
Unthinkable within the boundaries
Of what's understood in this relationship
Resulting in admissions of affection, anguish
And the value of human connection
Despite the alienating mode of interaction
Which they address during this conversation
As well as the fact that they've never actually met
She confesses she may take a job in Miami
She's on a layover in Dulles airport
He drives out to the airport, walks into a kitschy bar, at the climax
In the final shot we see them driving back into the city together
That's the end
As of now I'm calling this screenplay *Happening Now*

Tomaž says either marry a sorceress or become homosexual
He's given it a lot of thought
There is no other way

When I look into the mirror
I see the possibilities
I don't know how it is for you
I'm going to deny
And expand
Like my sorrow isn't good enough
There will always be new stuff to buy
Winona Ryder levitating
At the end of Beetlejuice
I think I should talk to her about all of this
She's probably thought about it a lot too
Child like the world
Why don't more people actually suicide
Glamour
Illusion
Human frailty
So tell me

persona. brand. empire. andré balazs (b. 1957) purchased the chateau marmont in 1990, at the start of a decade known as the longest period of peacetime economic expansion. personal incomes doubled from what they were during the recession in 1990. after the 1996 welfare reform act the united states experienced a reduction of poverty. the wall street stock exchange stayed over the 10,500 mark from 1999 to 2001. during this time, balazs expanded his hotel collection when he purchased and restored the mercer hotel in downtown new york, establishing "the benchmark by which other fashionable design hotels would come to be judged." the andré balazs luxury group's holdings now include chateau marmont in hollywood and sunset beach on shelter island. the standard hotel locations include hollywood, downtown la, miami beach, high line, meatpacking district and the newest addition, the standard, east village. in 2011, balazs launched a sea plane service to the hamptons, StndAIR, an 8 seat plane operating scheduled flights and charters from manhattan. this summer, andré balazs is pleased to release two new labels of his andré balazs collection of rosé. an international blend in collaboration with château minuty, located in the provence region of france, and a second, sunset beach rosé, being produced in partnership with the local winery on long island's east end. more a resort than cosmopolitan hotel, the sunset beach location includes a lively french beachside restaurant and bar with sunset views and a luxury beach boutique. international hotel staff are on hand to assist in arranging all the local activities. do you like drinking wine?

if you can't afford it, affect it. known for its romantic small homes characterized by a low, broad frame building with end gables with a large central chimney, the cape cod house is synonymous with new england romance, designed to withstand the stormy, stark weather of the massachusetts coast, that thin curve of land in an infinite black sea. during winter, darkness so wholly encapsulates the cape, residents say it qualifies to have its own time zone to account for the premature sunsets over the cape's drastically eastward bound longitude. its famous icy clear skies rendered into devastating sunsets. the cape and islands regional suicide prevention coalition was formed in 2009 after statistics proved suspicions in cape cod were true: short days and long quiet dark nights correlated with high suicide rates. spring also appears notoriously delayed each year despite cape cod's high average of 200+ sunny days per year.

andrew sends me a warhol quote: warhol's asked "do you believe in emotions?" and responds "yes, unfortunately I have them." andrew has an extra ticket to paul mccarthy's ws show at the armory so i attend with him. it is july of 2013. 100 degrees. 21st century. later in the evening i cool off reading reviews of the show and wonder if a white man can can ethically portray female exploitation and alterity, (meaning *could i?*) in the times review they relate the thematic content partly as determining nostalgia as a fool's faith. the times, in a separate but much longer article on frank ocean's rise to international fame, agree that maybe it is best for artists to give less when speaking publicly about their work. frank ocean's debut mixtape *nostalgia*, ultra was released free despite being signed to island / def jam who delayed movement on a release during the first few years he was under contract. *nostalgia, ultra* apprehends the past as source material on which to graft emotions. the cover to *nostalgia, ultra*, designed by ocean himself, features an early '90s model bmw m3 in neon orange, parked at the forest hedge. *channel orange*, his follow-up album, for which he was paid a million dollars in advance, exhibits a pure swatch of the same orange tone.

these pure, "natural" colors express instinctual life and threaten inwardness. look around inside a bed, bath and beyond some time: gray, garnet, mauve, beige. reassuring certitudes for the anxious subject. in this regard bright color becomes apprehended on products as a sign of emancipation—often compensating in the home for the absence of more fundamental qualities (particularly a lack of space). the preserve® bpa-free pasta strainer in "ripe tomato" or "apple green." cuisinart® dutch ovens in "provencal blue" "island spice red" or "pumpkin." having once represented something approaching a liberation, both have now become signs that are merely traps, raising the banner of freedom but delivering none to direct experience.

bpa, a man-made synthetic compound found in certain plastics, introduced into the mainstream by bayer and general electric in the 1950s, found now in products such as 99¢ disposable water bottles and other temporary food storage containers, has been reported to affect neurological functions and behavior. to avoid bpa, you'll want to avoid number 7 plastics, which as containers leach bpa as they break down over time, heat up in in the microwave, or are subject to hot water during cleaning. one way to avoid bpa is to use a stainless steel water bottle (like the klean kanteens carried right here at bed bath and beyond). and now on shelves are klean kanteen's new advanced design sport cap 2.0, which has a loop, dust cover and sport top. very convenient, very klean and very cute (see?).

kate moss saint tropez no tan lines. the huffington post reported that individuals engaging in bdsm sex suffer less anxiety and emjoy greater well-being than others. july emotional heat index. diamonds fur coat champagne. totally gorgeous sunsets. netflix under the drone of box fans. air conditioners reportedly in peak use on weekdays at 6pm. watching television online and wondering if my fashion has become normative and cinematic. when you start by imagining what it might be like, you step back, you think. how it makes someone feel. the experience of the product. this is what matters. this is it.

it's the year of the snake, and an elegant dress, bag, or shoe is one of the easiest ways to incorporate it into your wardrobe. an alluring pit of python sheath dresses and clutches is on the market right now. wearing just one serpentine element makes for a memorable look. click through for examples of this stunning trend, picks for pre-fall, the latest in berlin street style, beauty, people, parties, culture. spears first performed "i'm a slave 4 u" publicly at the 2001 mtv video music awards at the metropolitan opera house in new york city on september 6, 2001. along with dancing in a very revealing outfit, the performance is probably most remembered for featuring a number of exotic animals, including a white tiger and a live albino burmese python on her shoulders, the latter of which has become one of spears' most iconic images. the inclusion of the animals in the performance brought a great deal of criticism from animal rights organization people for the ethical treatment of animals (peta). in august 2008, the mtv network named the performance the most memorable moment in vma history.

i wake up at 4:30 a.m. i never really sleep much and often start my day at this time. when i am very lucky and sleep through the night, i might get up at 7:00, but that is rare. the first thing i do when i get out of bed is weigh myself. i do this every morning, and if i have gained more than two or three pounds, i try to eat fruit and vegetables exclusively for a couple of days until my weight is back to my ideal. i make myself a tall glass of iced espresso (i don't like warm drinks), get into a hot bath, and slowly sip my drink as i come to life.

if you can't live off your wage, consider living at work. more than 20 percent of new yorkers may be living in poverty, the country may be on the verge of another war in the middle east, but this year's fash-ion week is turning out to be a weeklong party for the ages, with so many events, hardly anyone can keep them straight. remember the chris dorner manhunt? remember shape-ups? remember jay z at pace gallery? remember the beginning of the recession of the american economy? people asked *would new york city be affected?* no, they'd say, it's too much of an international city.

i was about to start a job at that time. the night before the first day in the office—well my mind just goes constantly—i took a sleeping pill, and had a dream that was really vivid. i was walking into my office for the first time. it seemed no one was there, it was possibly a saturday and my desk was near the very back of the floor. it was quiet, the floors were vacuumed, everything was untouched. the halls continued for quite some time. the serenity of it had a pristine purity. i thought *you know, i feel like i've been here before*. far back there was the glow of a desk lamp, in an office that look liked it might be mine. i turned and followed the path. within an hour i came into the office and there was an individual slumped back in the desk chair—myself—like i had been there thousands of years.

i thought about chelsea manning for a long time again yesterday, and then again as i was drifting asleep last night. today i decide she's become allegorical of nearly 100 years of failed western culture, and in fact, likely the most important story and person of the postmodern era. born the second child of a squarely nuclear family, her father traveled while her british mother, who didn't drive, spent her days drinking. after their divorce, manning relocated to wales, where she became the target of bullying for being american and, living as a boy, for being viewed as effeminate. her mother's decaying mental health lead chelsea back to the united states to live with her father in oklahoma city, where she had violent confrontations with her stepmother over her troubled employment status. manning left for tulsa in a truck given to her by her father, sleeping in it at first, then moving in with a high school friend, whom she briefly worked with in a themed all-you-can-eat pizza buffet called *incredible pizza*. chelsea soon after settled in with an aunt in potomac, maryland, for a 15 month period of stability while working, leisurely attending school, and dating. manning enlisted in the military in 2007 with plans to attend college through the g.i. bill. she told her army supervisor later that she had also hoped joining a masculine environment would resolve her gender identity. trapped beneath the totalizing censorship of *don't ask, don't tell*, and opposed to the kind of war in which she found herself involved, in january 2010 she began posting on facebook that she felt hopeless and alone. subjected to solitary confinement after arrest, denied pardon after conviction, chelsea manning had the perfectly uncomplicated goal of "revealing the true nature of 21st century asymmetric warfare." coming out as transgender tazed the nation's media, unable to mature themselves to the contemporary politics of identification, most media outlets continuing to use the "he" despite the perfectly clear "i am chelsea manning, i am female" declaration. never on her own terms. sweet child from oklahoma.

court-ordered chemical castration became legalized in 2033. cyproterone acetate was combined with an anti-psychotic medication; sex offenders had wrist sleeves procedurally implanted which deposited the hormone inhibiting serum directly into the bloodstream via reverse iontophoresis processes. lack of funding for prisons led to shorter sentencing, but the convicted wore sleeves for life. everything was tracked. airlines merged into a symbolic oligarchy of parent companies. borders locked in cold wars fought over the last remaining fossil fuels. civilian travel applications lolled around bureaucratic networks. the rich traveled through a privately administered network of jets. the poor went unmonitored. international markets governed the wealthy. in 2043 the death penalty became nationalized under the flag. those sentenced were hauled to one of four national zones on the 1st of each month. contractors streamed the executions. after scotus passed the "treason act," journalists became extinct. encrypted news traveled through torrents, a moving target for the administration. in a macabre act of political theatre, suri cruise, operating out of a digital commune of leftists, dropouts, artists and hackers, founded the "funeral party." in families, suicides among siblings or kin were encouraged by a series of income tax waivers. families of euthanized elders collected payouts and substantial debt relief. amounts were determined on an age gradient. in time, cruise's gesture quietly became right wing legislature under the staid auspice of the "family care and protection act." the middle class rose from the grave.

you look good, like the ads. continuously reconstituted through the things i desire. because i want things and need to be desired. when they say "we're being authentic," they mean "we're extremely on message." a content warning. a user history. i understand and wish to continue. i'm going in late to work today. and i'll probably be coming home late. love you, so sorry, dear. a tax form. a loan application. the eighteenth brumaire of louis bonaparte. may be monitored. viva la vida. a whitening treatment. become a friend and save 30% today. shop the entire store.

L'OFFICIEL HOMMES

dev hynes

you smell like summer

in the tropics

your new car

smells like cocaine

mustique rain

slanting downward

on a hilfiger towel

i miss summer

in greece

eating grapes

depressed economies

desultory poetics

everything is embarrassing

century 21

a savings account

dev hynes

enunciate pleasures

i still feel

pleasures of empire

bourgeois pleasures of time

authenticating details

a paris autumn

a new starbucks in dubai

egyptian cotton

bananes frites

losing you

on location in st. barth

a video look book

a sunset view

we shared a sandwich

on a balcony

in montreal

it was april

i was slow

with my camera

dev hynes

it was warm

after winter

you said

feel the world

against your skin

in the parc

du mont-royal

among the many people

we bought

opium and hash

and smoked it

near the basilica

from a pipe

carved from marble

in the shape

of a mollusk

because lord is dead

and grace existential

songs set to feelings

songs of empire

dev hynes

a melody

dev hynes

after hours

dev hynes

dev hynes

dev hynes

on the cover

dev hynes

1280 X 768, 60HZ

John and Mary meet.
What happens next?

A.

They flirt through text and social media, grafting their lust onto a
tenuous mutual experience they shared at Avenue in the Meatpack-
ing District during a mutual friend's birthday: someone bumps
into Mary, causing her to spill vodka onto her handbag a moment
before John is introduced to her. She remains lighthearted about
it, so the misfortune becomes the topic of their conversation. John
dabs the orange leather clutch with cocktail napkins and orders a
replacement drink. Because they're New Yorkers, they discuss the
neighborhoods they live in, what they do for work, and where they
like to hang out. John studied business, lives in the East Village and
works for a digital media company, Mary studied psychology, lives
in Tribeca and consults for an online shopping website. They share
music and food as hobbies. Mary enjoyed the recent Diego Rivera
exhibition, which John hadn't seen. John had always believed he
would own a business, and they laugh at how, just 5 years ago, they
wouldn't have imagined being on the career path they currently
follow. John loves craft beer, and writes articles "for obnoxious
partying males," as he puts it. Mary's clients don't follow trends,
but instead are devoted to unique or high fashion. As dutiful and
educated employees whose work only benefits a detached board
of owners, what else are they to do but ironize their existence?
They like going to brunch, though John had that day just bought
equipment to brew pour-over style coffee which he was eager to
try. The next morning they both did. And maybe that first night at
home, his head between her legs, Mary moaning with pleasure,
John saw into the future. Check-in for a free appetizer. Traceable
spending habits. Human behavior indicating a belief that the world

has already ended. Their affective decision-making acknowledges no linearity, making John and Mary normative consumer models regarding their shifting sense of morality vis-à-vis nihilistic indulgence. They're just like us. John comes into money after his father dies, and he purchases an apartment in a luxury condo building they watched being built. They move in together and become engaged, wedding a year later. Mary wants a child. Six months into their marriage John discovers he has a low sperm count, though treatments are available. After two years of no luck they accept their lot. Now age 31, Mary begins spending more time away from John, staying out late drinking with co-workers or friends she met at a continued learning course on wine, or taking the car alone on weekends to visit her mother in Pennsylvania. Soon after, she moves out and asks for divorce. John takes a job managing assets for a bank in New Jersey and relocates to Montclair. After two years Mary is living with a boyfriend in Lancaster. John and Mary don't really speak.

B.

He doesn't get the job, but thanks her for the chance to talk in a follow up email. A few months later they run into each other at a pool party in Echo Park. He has since found employment as a copywriter at a similar agency and plans on staying indefinitely. She confides they hired the niece of a board member, who has already left the company for another job. Mary has another party to go to and asks John to find her online. John does, and they are able to learn about each other's social habits, friend group, eating patterns and lifestyle, and occasionally comment on each other's activity, though they never see each other in real life again.

C.

John and Mary enjoy a passionate relationship for many years, living together in Montreal. John is a novelist, teaching literature in a college. Mary is a very successful commercial producer working in advertising. One day, after doing laundry together, John comes out to Mary as transgender. She reacts poorly, accusing John of being gay. John, now known as Jesse, says she has been living a lie her entire life and needs to restart in order to thrive. Against the wishes of her family, Mary agrees to give it a try, becoming a big supporter of Jesse while helping her adapt to the nuances of clothing and makeup. Their honeymoon period is tested when Jesse loses her position at the college over concerns about her transition. Mary discovers she is pregnant, though doesn't make a disclosure to Jesse, and succumbs to depression after secretly having an abortion. She leaves Jesse, ultimately marrying and having a child with a man. Jesse begins dating and moves in with her girlfriend Madge, though remains deeply in love with Mary, "the love of her life." Jesse sends Mary a copy of her new book, whose themes and symbolic disclosures resonate with Mary and convince her to agree to a tryst with Jesse, under the cover story of working on a commercial on the desolate and romantic Isle of Black. They spend the weekend with a post-op trans couple, and Mary is once again unable to cope with the realities of life with a trans woman. They fight, and Mary confesses the abortion to Jesse. They part ways once again. Despite being homeless, childless, middle-aged and loveless, Jesse thrives as an award-winning author, and continues publishing. In a lengthy newspaper feature, stable and relatively secure, Jesse feels proud to age as a woman. In a daytime meeting in a Montreal bar during a leafy autumn, ten years after their first break up, Mary teases Jesse for living a life suspended above the ground with her thoughts in the sky. Jesse reacts defensively, and they have a brief but serious conversation exemplary of the disharmony that troubled their relationship as Mary was never able to comfortably accept living her life with who Jesse truly is. Jesse exits the bar alone after paying the bill while Mary is in the bathroom.

D.

They sing karaoke and really seem to like each other, John going so far as to think an unseen force brought them together over a mutual love of music they discovered in the elevator at work. Talking together late one night with friends, Mary says she doesn't believe in true love, a discussion that becomes the primary obsession of their relationship. Turns out, in this story, that John is correct, but they are an inappropriate match. Their patchy fling ends as Mary meets a new man for whom she genuinely feels lust, affection, and intellectual affinities. John limps into a new relationship with a woman named Jane as autumn begins.

E.

They begin a powerful affair, like birds caught in a thermal, from a very young age. Never marrying on principle, though effectively life partners, John and Mary live out a happy, dedicated relationship well into their thirties. Mary, visiting a fertility doctor after "having trouble," and feeling ill from the stress of trying to conceive, discovers that not only is she infertile, but after a series of referrals and ongoing tests, she learns she's got stage IV stomach cancer. Her condition isn't operable. John and Mary are devastated. John discovers a treatment—gray market—being developed in Switzerland, an artificially intelligent organic cell structure called Accellate, which attacks and eradicates harmful cells, regenerating body tissue and cell mass. Not much is known about it. They risk it all. John and Mary disinherit themselves of life as they've lived it. Six months later Mary is healed and virile, essentially in the dawn of her existence. Years pass pleasantly, they celebrate milestones in their relationship. Putting aside Mary's ongoing desire for children, they decide to embrace their union as an end-in-itself. John celebrates his 50th birthday. Mary has ceased to age. She's taken to a diet of raw foods, green juice, yoga. She keeps a low profile making house visits for under-the-table body work in Orange County, while John has stabilized their income, making investments in the tech industry. Called to Zurich for a 20-year study of Accellate patients, John and Mary's observations are acknowledged: Mary's body isn't decaying. Versions of Accellate have been developed to function in a more organic mode, though physicians plan to proceed with what they've seemingly discovered: the tonic for eternal youth. Testimonies are being prepared with a team of lawyers. They tell Mary and John they have a celebrity spokesman who has since received Accellate and is ready to make a bold public announcement. Meanwhile, the International Court of Justice subpoenas the physicians for malpractice for their unregulated testing on humans. Mary and John settle the terms of a payout and move to Tangier. While Mary thrives, John sinks into a deep depression as he passes through middle age. Mary begins taking lovers. Men's sexual enhancement medicine carries them through the onset of erectile dysfunction in John's fifties. Failing that, in desperation, he has surgically implanted a hydraulic, inflatable prosthesis which Mary immediately rejects. John grows old, now so obviously a mismatch, their relationship purely platonic. The day before John's 72nd birthday, at a hotel on the Bay of Tangier, John discovers Mary is 4 months pregnant and plans to have the child. The next morning John wakes before Mary and watches the sunset one last time from the edge of the bluffs, then enacts the conclusive end of his life, as he lived it, with Mary.

THE LINE OF BEAUTY

I love summer, the luxury of poetry, gin
and tonic, quinine lost in juniper

ACKNOWLEDGMENTS

Some of these poems have appeared in *Action Yes, Atlas Review, Birds of Lace, Boston Review, Brooklyn Poets, Bushwick Sweethearts, Coconut, Destroyer, Everyday Genius, Finery, Heartcloud, Imperial Matters, Maggy, notnostrums, Similar:Peaks::, Souvenir, Sprung Formal, Third Rail,* and *The Volta.* "Conscripts of Modernity" appeared in *Privacy Policy: An Anthology of Surveillance Poetics,* published by Black Ocean.

"Like" and "Sunset" were previously published in the chapbook *Cool Memories* (Spork). "Fantasy", "Odalisque", "Flâneur", "Los Angeles", "#nofilter skies", "sno-cone", and "girlwithcat2.jpg" were previously published in the chapbook *Odalisque* (Bloof Books).

"Mexicali Twinks" was commisioned by *Animal* as part of a "Porn Poetry" feature, where artists were invited to generate poems based on a PornMD livestream showing search terms in real time.

"1280 x 768, 60Hz" exists in gratitude to Margaret Atwood's *Happy Endings.*

Thanks to the following people for various amounts of support and editorial oversight: Monica McClure, Andrew Durbin, Kate Durbin, Alli Warren, Macgregor Card, Sasha Fletcher, Becca Klaver, Dan Magers, Jennifer Tamayo, Brandon Brown, Dana Ward, Andrew Shuta, Audrey Zee Whitesides, Ariana Reines.

Special thanks to Juliana Spahr, without whose encouragement this manuscript would not have been completed.

Thank you to Matvei Yankelevich, Michael Newton, and Anna Moschovakis at UDP.